# HOW TO TAKE ON THE I.R.S. AND WIN

*<u>Strategic Tips</u>*
*To get out and stay out of tax trouble!*

By
Alexander Howard
Enrolled Agent

**I.R.S. Troubleshooters**
P.O. Box 18101
Anaheim Hills, CA 92807
(714) 283-8702
e-mail: irstrobl@ix.netcom.com

Copyright © 1997 by Alexander Howard

All rights reserved. No part of this book may be reproduced or transmitted in any form or by any means, electronic or mechanical, including photocopying, recording, or any information storage and retrieval system, without permission in writing from the Publisher.

ISBN 0-9637863-7-7

# Introduction

Darnell Boone's older brother pushed him into me. I pushed him back. We grabbed each other and the fight was on. This fight had been months in the making. We were both twelve. He was from Magnolia. I was from the more upscale Pierce Park. Boys the same age from Pierce Park and Magnolia fought each other. Whoever lost the fight would be socially inferior to the boy who won.

Darnell and I wrestled our way into a ditch. He had me by the neck upside down and wouldn't let go.

My older brother Eugene, hoping to see a more active fight, made Darnell let go of me. I got out of the ditch and walked towards Darnell who had his fists up ready to fight. I stuck out my hand to shake his.

"We're even," I told him and walked away. I was not afraid of Darnell. But I wasn't mad at him either. To me, being from a different neighborhood was not a good reason to fight.

The decision to walk away from the fight with Darnell has served me well in the thirty-four years since it happened. I only fight in genuine self-defense. And when I do fight, I fight to win.

When I take on the I.R.S., I don't get mad. Neither should you. I get busy—busy finding the administrative mistakes and misapplications of the tax laws that invariably abound when an I.R.S. agent deliberately hurts a taxpayer. To me, that's a good enough reason to fight.

Any I.R.S. agent or taxpayer who chooses to act out of anger will most likely make decisions that don't square up with the reasoning of tax codes or I.R.S. procedures. The I.R.S. as a system is designed so agents who abuse their considerable powers can be stopped. But the legal protection you have is only good if you know how to use it. The unwritten rule in

## Introduction

dealing with an abusive I.R.S. agent is: don't get mad, get busy.

Tax trouble is to be expected for any taxpayers I.R.S. agents suspect of cheating. Yet a more insidious form of abuse goes unnoticed by honest taxpayers who don't understand how sweet the tax law system really is on honest, financially productive taxpayers.

The circumstances I write about are largely concerned with self-defense against unwarranted I.R.S. tax trouble. Invariably such insights lead to an understanding essential to maximize the benefits written into the tax code for taxpayers who play the game fairly.

*Alexander Howard*

How to Take On the I.R.S. and Win

# Contents

I. Tax Trouble ............................... 9

II. Anatomy of Tax Trouble ...................... 17

III. The Human Side of the I.R.S. ................. 55

IV. What to Do When an I.R.S. Agent Plays Dirty .... 93

    Profile: Alexander Howard ................... 101

    Some Keys to I.R.S. Administrative File Jargon ... 103

How to Take On the I.R.S. and Win

# 1
# Tax Trouble

The I.R.S. is a public service agency of the federal government with the responsibility to assess and collect the correct amount of income tax for each tax-paying situation. The agency wants what you legally owe. Nothing more. Certainly nothing less. Many of the I.R.S. horror stories you hear about happen because the agent responsible for the situation believes the taxpayer is guilty of a crime or is willfully negligent in paying an assessed tax liability. Even if the agent happens to be wrong, the burden of proof is on you, the taxpayer. More burdensome than the proof can be getting anyone in the I.R.S. to listen to you when you're this deep into tax trouble.

The I.R.S. has a large number of employees whose

job it is to resolve taxpayers' disputes with agents. Some of these employees have workloads similar to the *Maytag Repairman* because the public doesn't understand how to benefit from their services.

It's been my experience that tax trouble comes in one of four ways. One, you deliberately deceived the I.R.S. and they've discovered the deed. At this point in tax trouble, the I.R.S. employees you encounter are not likely to display that friendly customer service attitude. Their behavior might be rude, or unethical; but unless you know that it should technically by law never be either, you wind up another victim of a flaw in the wheels of tax justice. The fruits of being caught deliberately cheating the I.R.S. can range from civil penalties to criminal prosecution and federal prison time.

Are there measures you can take to lessen the blow should you find yourself in tax trouble because an I.R.S. agent suspects you of deliberately evading the correct amount of income taxes? Yes. But if you're wrong and you know you're wrong, the less you make the agent work to clear the case from his or her inventory, the better off you are. More planets would have to line up than it takes to bring about a messiah for you to challenge and win a case like this against the I.R.S. Yet if you genuinely don't agree with the I.R.S.'s take on your business or life circumstances, you have to be able to show that what the I.R.S. agent suspects of you is not true.

A second way into tax trouble is when honest mistakes that favor the government are found on tax returns. Taxpayers faced with this kind of trouble can still face civil penalties, interest and additional tax liabilities unless these are challenged administratively.

A financially damaging, third kind of tax trouble results when life or business circumstances are not adequately reflected in tax returns. When accurate tax-related information is not communicated to the I.R.S., it can lead to financial ruin through tax liens, levies, seizures of property and bankruptcy. The most widespread kind of tax trouble I've encountered to date has come to honest taxpayers who've cheated themselves out of income tax dollars they are legally entitled to keep. This kind of tax trouble goes largely undetected and the vast majority of its victims never know they're having trouble. There are estimated to be over 7,000,000 people, partnerships and corporations who file tax returns yearly with errors and omissions that cause them to pay more income taxes than legally necessary. The overpayments routinely range in the hundreds, thousands and in some cases millions of dollars. The overpaying tax returns pass the I.R.S.'s scrutiny because they don't look for tax returns that might be paying too much. I've never known them to have a problem refunding money shown to be legitimately due but the I.R.S. error detection mechanisms are directed at the people who might underpay their taxes.

The last and least likely way of getting into tax trouble is when a report is made to the I.R.S. by someone you've angered or when their systemic bird dog comes upon your scent while it's sniffing another taxpayer.

Unlike the criminal justice system, when the I.R.S. accuses you, the presumption is of your guilt until you prove your innocence. If you don't know how to cope, hire someone to independently audit your life and business circumstances in search of tax return communication errors. This is the bottom line of all tax trouble, correctly communicating the tax related circumstances to the I.R.S. If the I.R.S. charges you with criminal fraud and you believe they are wrong, have a tax advisor with I.R.S. audit experience review your records and advise you and your attorney before you prepare your defense. This gives you the additional perspective of seeing beforehand how the I.R.S. is likely to see your situation based on your records. Practitioners who have not been an I.R.S. audit agent might not have the kind of inside knowledge of I.R.S. internal procedure to summarize your position.

There are procedural strategies available to you when the I.R.S. is only proposing civil penalties and interest. You can agree to the proposed adjustments of your tax liability. This closes your case with no criminal prosecution or penalties for that given tax return. Once the I.R.S. issues a civil report they cannot then change their minds and seek criminal penalties for the same issues. Actually, the same thing happens if you ignore all the civil notices and never show up. The case then closes as a "no show audit." It takes a lot longer and 12% interest on the taxes and the penalties continue to mount for what can sometimes be years.

There is also the option of going through with the audit and challenging the I.R.S.'s proposed adjustment. This would be wise only if you can document a significant amount of the items the I.R.S. is questioning you on. Thereafter the I.R.S. supposedly scrutinizes your returns more closely for the items they challenged you on and won. Where the I.R.S. challenges you and you prevail, audit procedures protect you from being challenged regarding the same issue again for several years, unless you were examined as a business.

## Tax Trouble

There is another important thing to remember. I.R.S. agents, notably auditors and revenue officers, are strategically vulnerable whenever you see them driven by rudeness or hostility. This is especially true if they fail to bring up and explain the tax law or procedure which underlies their decisions and actions. If an agent is arrogant or otherwise out of control emotionally and psychologically, they are likely to make mistakes that can be used to your advantage.

How to Take On the I.R.S. and Win

# II
# ANATOMY OF TAX TROUBLE

I.R.S. agents have enormous power when it comes to your tax liability. That's not likely to change. My purpose is to present ways to get the agents you deal with to use their power to help instead of hurt you.

When you are presented with a proposal to adjust your tax liability, please remember that a proposal is just that—a proposal. Not a final decision. An I.R.S. agent has reviewed your tax return, supposedly studied the relevant laws and decided you owe the government more money for income taxes. If you don't agree and can justify your disagreement through your circumstances and documentation, you can walk away a winner with the I.R.S. agent's blessing. The agent's decision is made based on his or her understanding of the tax laws and your business or personal circumstances. Sometimes the agent's decision comes as a result of not having information on all relevant circumstances and can be remedied simply by providing such information to the agent. An agent's interpretation of the code and regulations can be based on misunderstanding and result in an erroneous decision against you. Fortunately the I.R.S. system has safeguards built into it to remedy such situations. However, safeguards, like fire exits, are only useful if you know about them.

Don't expect the I.R.S. to screen your tax records for errors which resulted in overpayment. There's a greater chance you'll hit the lottery than be notified by the I.R.S. that you've paid them too much.

The I.R.S. does, however, provide information which explains deductions, credits and allowances that reduce the amount of taxable income.

The federal tax laws favor the productive—people who are deliberately taking the kinds of risks which could lead to financial rewards. Skill at relating information to people and knowing the right people to get

## Anatomy of Tax Trouble

your information to is critical when circumstances lead to tax trouble. Again, how well your business or life circumstances are communicated to the I.R.S. very definitely influences how much you pay in income taxes.

Sob stories that have no bearing on tax liabilities will fall on deaf ears but genuine tax related hardship circumstances like financial losses, earthquake damage and thefts can carry a lot of clout when you're trying to claw your way out of tax trouble. If you or your representative is not willing to work at making sure the I.R.S. completely understands your business or personal circumstances, you will almost certainly pay them more than is legally required.

Sometimes, to gain a legitimate tax advantage, it becomes necessary to fight the I.R.S. for it. The tax professional or private citizen who approaches this fight armed only with a technical know how can be in for a very frustrating experience. The interaction with the agent has a tremendous impact on how much you pay in taxes. Not many other situations in life present the possibilities of such tangible rewards.

The human element is naturally prominent in tax trouble, even tax trouble that is technically off base. To fail to anticipate this is to ask for trouble. One way to ensure a positive outcome to your tax trouble is being able to back up your claims with a paper trail. Present your evidence with clarity, confidence and code sections to back you up. Read everything you can get your hands on about the situation you find yourself in. Free I.R.S. pamphlets and publications may do the trick. The information in simple language shows you how to correctly and legally take advantage of tax loopholes. Public libraries are good sources of I.R.S. information. The I.R.S. provides a phone number you can call and request free information regarding any aspect of tax law that relates to your circumstances.

I.R.S. agents you come in contact with are duty-bound to tell you of laws that favor you. But don't count on it to happen, though. For one thing, the agent may not know the laws that favor you. The scope of an I.R.S. examination might very well not consider the uniqueness of your business or personal circumstances and how these might influence tax liability. You might have to point them out. A single agent's decision can more often than not carry the force of judge, jury and executioner when by law it shouldn't. If you have a different point of view and can substantiate your position, the I.R.S. is bound by law to consider your evidence. When faced with an agent's determination of your tax liability, you are confronted with another human being's judgment of what the tax laws relating to your situation mean. In criminal justice cases there must be proof beyond a reasonable doubt. In I.R.S. cases the proof need not go beyond an individual agent's doubt for an additional tax liability to be assessed.

Tax problems can occur because certain taxpayers want nothing to do with the I.R.S. They take their papers to their accountant and write out a check for what he or she says they owe. This attitude towards dealing with the I.R.S. is a sure sign a person is playing the game to lose. All of the people I've ever known who paid too much for income taxes, blindly trusted the determination of their tax liability to someone else.

In an I.R.S. audit the examiner is not only challenging the integrity of your records. Your personal integrity is under scrutiny as well. Good books and records don't always mean elaborate, double-entry accounting systems. Receipts saved in an old shoe box are acceptable if they are organized and show a clear paper trail of your tax circumstances. The better the paper trail, the smoother your road through encounters with I.R.S. agents.

There are times when subjective issues have an influence over an agent's decision and even with good books and records, I.R.S. nightmare cases happen. Like any public servant, I.R.S. agents may be swayed by prejudice, envy or lust when passing judgment on your tax liability. But never let the absence of good books and records stop you from fighting for a deduction you believe in your heart to be a correct entitlement. There are laws such as the Cohan Rule, which allows you to take tax deductions for items that you may not have records to substantiate.

The following three stories illustrate what should and what can happen in an I.R.S. audit.

I called out the taxpayer's name. An elderly gentleman stood up from his seat, smiled and was about to extend his hand to shake mine. I turned abruptly, pretending not to notice his hand.

"Follow me, please." I walked deliberately while crowding the narrow passageway to my cubicle. I made certain he could not walk beside or in front of me. This was to set the tone early that I was in control of this situation. There is solid logic behind the auditor remaining in control. I knew where the interview needed to go to get the job done and avoid causing him any more grief than necessary.

"Have a seat." I said blandly, pointing to the two chairs with their backs jammed close to the wall. He took a seat. His knees had just a few inches clearance from the front of my battleship-gray metal desk. I handed him a copy of the Taxpayer Bill of Rights.

"I'm going to do an examination of your tax returns and records from the year 1991." I began filling out my required paperwork while I spoke, careful not to look directly at him. "Any information you give me or that I discover about you is protected by the Privacy Act. The only way anyone gets information about you is if you give me written permission. I will use any information I obtain to determine your correct tax liability. If I make an adjustment to your federal tax liability then we automatically notify the state of California about the federal adjustments. Any questions?"

Like almost everybody I've ever audited, he didn't ask me any questions so I proceeded with the audit.

"What exactly do you do for a living, sir?"

"O-on weekends I'm a drag racer."

I knew he had to be joking, but I was not about to laugh until I knew whether or not he was cheating. I re-stated my question.

"I mean what do you do to make money?"

The bearded, elderly gentleman became defensive.

"What right do you have to tell me what I can do? You know, you might be discriminating against me because of my age."

That's when I knew it was not going to be a routine audit.

I put my pencil down.

"How old are you, sir?"

"Seventy-four." he said.

A blind man could have seen my skepticism.

"You drive a drag racer for a living?"

He responded defiantly, "You got some kind of problem with that?"

I leaned back in my chair and locked my hands

behind my head.

"When and where do you drive this race car?"

The bearded man stuck his chest out.

"Every weekend. As you can see, I don't make a lot of money doing it."

Auditors are expected to examine the circumstances of taxpayers' lives. What they discover is used to make judgment calls about how much the taxpayer owes the government for taxes. This taxpayer's low reported income of $750, the deductions of $16,875, and my feeling that he was lying about being a race driver were already enough to disallow his deductions. I wondered how far he was going with his story.

"Do you own the car?"

"Yes," he said proudly.

"May I see the purchase documents for the vehicle?"

He handed me the paperwork. I read over the registration papers.

"You race a 1976 Volvo station wagon?"

"Uh... I... uh, do you know the race they have in

Long Beach every year?"

I struggled to keep from laughing.

"You ran the Long Beach Grand Prix in a Volvo Station Wagon?"

"No. But they have races like that every weekend in Pomona."

I laughed out loud.

"Are you trying to hustle me?"

The taxpayer's face took on a worried expression as he sat back in his chair. He managed a weak smile.

"It was try or die. You caught me. What are you going to do, put me in jail?"

I had won for the I.R.S., but something didn't feel right. I pretended not to hear him and silently studied the tax return while trying to get in touch with what I was feeling. I noticed because of his 1099s for interest, dividends and pensions, he had invested wisely when he was a younger man.

The taxpayer broke the silence.

"I figure I've done my share, you know? I've paid taxes since I was sixteen years old. All the government does is waste it anyway. I just don't think it's right that I've got to pay so much at my age."

I glanced up at him and could see the pain in his face. The face reminded me of my own retired father's face when something was really bothering him. It was evident to me that he honestly believed he'd been paying too much for taxes. It caused me to examine his return more thoroughly to see if he was right. I spotted the amount of money he'd paid into his IRAs over the years.

"Have you recovered your contributions to these IRAs?"

"What?" He frowned.

I was scribbling some notes and looking through his other documents.

"I'll explain it later," I told him. "Where does the life insurance distribution come from?"

The taxpayer looked down at the floor. "My wife passed away last year. It comes from her job." He leaned over my desk to see what I was writing. His hands trembled. "What are you writing?"

I held up my hand as a gesture for him to wait.

He sat quietly until I finished writing. When I finished I looked up at him.

"I'm going to disallow all of your Schedule C race car deductions."

He looked worried.

"What's that going to cost me?"

Since he didn't show up for the audit with a chip on his shoulder and I didn't have to battle with him, I wanted to try and help him.

"You are entitled to recover the cost of your IRA distributions, to use the death benefits exclusion and to take a retirement credit deduction on Schedule R."

I started crunching numbers on my calculator and writing out the audit report.

"Young man, I have no idea what all that stuff you said means."

This particular taxpayer honestly believed he was paying the I.R.S. too much money for taxes. The difference between him and millions of other people in the same boat was his luck that day. He had deducted items to which he was not legally entitled. Fortunately, the tax savings for the legal deductions were less than $50 short of what had been illegally deducted on his tax return. "No harm, no foul." The I.R.S. will not attempt to collect a liability of $50 or less. Even if he had encountered an agent who would have considered his actions to be tax fraud, the I.R.S. as a rule would not attempt to indict or prosecute someone his age for tax fraud unless that someone happened to have celebrity status.

When the I.R.S. deals harshly with tax cheaters, they are not trying to instill fear in all taxpayers. Just the dishonest ones. The I.R.S. is not shy about playing hardball with people they catch cheating on their taxes. But to those taxpayers who voluntarily play by the rules, the I.R.S. wears a different, oftentimes caring and helpful game face.

The I.R.S. in reality is a fluid entity. It changes personnel and procedures frequently. To get out of tax trouble often requires direct contact with an I.R.S. employee. Let's say you have a technically sound position on an issue, yet you're not able to get your point across to the I.R.S. agent. It's time to inform the agent that you wish to discuss the situation with a supervisor. The I.R.S. has procedural remedies in place to resolve technical disputes between the public and I.R.S. employees. Personality conflicts between agents and the public are another matter.

In a relationship, one human being has made a connection with another. This is true whether the relationship is a long-term marriage or a greeting to a stranger in passing. What determines the character of the relationship is the connection that is made. We live in a time of ATMs, the Home Shopping Network, drive-through windows and electronic mail. Relating constructively to another human being is rapidly declining as a factor in our daily lives. Yet, never is the ability to relate to other people more essential than when one deals with the I.R.S. The connection you make with the agent you encounter often determines the result of the encounter. Unfortunately, racism and other biases may influence the connection you make with the I.R.S. agent before you ever walk in the door.

I became involved with a case in the Laguna Niguel district because the taxpayers, who are Mexican-American, believed the auditor had discriminated against them.

The auditor had disallowed deductions for property taxes and business use of the home, among others. I examined the documents the taxpayers had presented to the auditor, then examined the auditor's workpapers. There was no legal justification for what the auditor had done. None. Nada. Who can tell what *ism* dictated this caucasian auditor's behavior? She certainly was not trying to assess the correct tax for the circumstances. It took nearly a year of going up the chain of command to Appeals to gain most of the deductions the taxpayers were legally entitled to.

Personality conflicts are difficult because they are most often hidden from the participants. People who are racist can't usually see that their behavior is colored

## SUPER CROWN #746

```
02/19/99  14:45   H      22    14833
REFUNDS WITHIN 30 DAYS WITH RECEIPT ONLY
         MAGAZINE SALES FINAL
    PUBLISHER            CROWN    CROWN
    PRICE                SAVINGS  PRICE
HT TAKE ON THE IRS & WI
   1@  15.95 0963786377   15%     13.56
SUBTOTAL                    $     13.56
SALES TAX @ 8.75%           $      1.19
TOTAL                       $     14.75
TENDERED CHARGE             $     14.75
6011300200526927  11/00 APPROVAL 019048

    YOUR SAVINGS AT CROWN... $ 2.39
```

## Anatomy of Tax Trouble

by their prejudice.

Proof of such prejudice is practically impossible to come by. The best approach is to attack what the agent has done. To attack the agent's credibility without clear and convincing evidence will only weaken your situation. When you attack actions, such as the disallowance of a depreciation deduction, this de-personalizes the situation and takes the human element out of the mix.

Sometimes it's easier to charm your way out of being dead wrong on a tax law issue than it is to be dead right and have the agent dislike you for some reason.

I've never met anyone who dreamed as a child of growing up to become an I.R.S. agent. It's a job. Like any other job, people come to it with a variety of skills, motives and stories about what got them there. They're not sadists or masochists, they're just people, and people are imperfect.

Tax trouble will be much less taxing on the psyche if you know the I.R.S. employees you meet will have no master computer which is connected to every other computer in the world and programmed with information about you. They are no less prone to the path of least resistance than any employee of a large corporation. Usually they only want to know as much about you as it takes to close your case and get you out of their caseload.

I once got involved in a client's collection case where another accountant was having trouble with an I.R.S. Agent. The previous accountant had suggested, in writing, that the Revenue Officer had been stealing checks the company had made out to the I.R.S. This accountant had made these unsubstantiated complaints to the I.R.S. National Office and a Congressman. The I.R.S. presented transcripts showing where the checks were applied to tax, penalties and interest. The former accountant, who was not a CPA, Enrolled Agent or attorney, wisely called in reinforcements when the I.R.S. was about to shut down the company and seize the assets to pay off the liability. The previous accountant had wasted time and energy with a baseless attack on the Revenue Officer's integrity. When this was so easily discredited, the accountant's integrity and competence were in question as well.

As an Enrolled Agent acting on the client's behalf, I approached the tax trouble from the angle of setting up a repayment agreement. The Revenue Officer had no personality conflict with me and respected my credentials as an Enrolled Agent trained by the I.R.S.

Another case comes to mind about tax trouble that came about because an I.R.S. agent took things too personally.

"Actually, my wife Morissa gave the church forty-five hundred dollars," George said, looking down at the floor. "But she says we shouldn't deduct it all so we won't get audited again."

I remember looking up from his tax records and frowning.

He looked like he was fighting back tears. "We were audited a couple of years ago. Because of our contributions."

I put the tax records down.

"What happened?"

George looked up from the floor. "I had the cancelled checks, plus we had a letter from the church."

"So why did they disallow it?"

George wiped his eyes with his shirt sleeve.

"The church's secretary happened to be my cousin." He shook his head. "The auditor was really tough. He wouldn't accept the letter from the church. He wouldn't allow our deductions for contributions."

I couldn't believe what I was hearing.

"Do you have cancelled checks written to the church?"

"Yes."

"For the year under audit?"

"Yes."

"And the auditor disallowed your contribution deduction because... how'd he know she was your cousin? And what difference does her being your cousin make?"

## Anatomy of Tax Trouble

George looked startled when I raised my voice and stood up.

"Do you still have the cancelled checks and the letter?"

"I've got most of them. Some of the money we gave in cash though." George smiled proudly. "We still give the money to the church but my wife doesn't want to report it. We give it in cash and don't report it because we don't want to get audited."

"Why didn't you challenge the auditor's decision?"

George gave me a thin smile.

"I went to the auditor's supervisor and all the way up to the Problems Resolution Office. The auditor's supervisor put me off and delayed the case just long enough to make me lose all my appeal rights."

George could have presented his evidence in any of three different ways: his actual source documents—the checks, the records of others who had requisite knowledge of the deductions, or by oral testimony. Rarely is oral testimony acceptable as the only means of verifying a tax benefit. But for contributions, a combination of your own records, cancelled checks, receipts and a raised-seal letter from a verifiable church makes oral testimony acceptable. The raised seal on church stationery is required for a good reason. As an auditor, I've come across phony church stationary used to verify false contributions. But George had copies of his cancelled checks made out to the church. If the contributions had been made out to the minister or any other person, the contributions deduction could be barred by the I.R.S. George's contribution deduction should have been accepted by the auditor. Seasoned auditors and appeals officers know the I.R.S. wouldn't have had a prayer in court with a case like this.

The auditor and his manager abused their positions by inhibiting George's legal appeal rights.

George could still get his money back in a number of different ways. He could pay the taxes, interest and penalties due, then file a claim for a refund on an amended return. The paid assessment would reinstate

George's appeal rights.

George's audit adjustments could have been protested through the Problems Resolution Office. His circumstances would certainly meet the criteria of someone who had gone through all the appropriate channels to resolve an I.R.S. problem.

George could also file an Offer In Compromise. An Offer In Compromise is a procedure where the taxpayer officially disagrees with the I.R.S. position on a tax liability.

The I.R.S. did not create George's problems. His own lack of knowledge did. He didn't have to accept the decision of the auditor or the auditor's manager. George's problem further developed because the I.R.S. people charged with the responsibility of enforcing the tax laws abused their positions. But the auditor's behavior was not representative of the I.R.S. as a system, any more than the behavior of rogue cops represent criminal justice as a whole.

The Martinezes are an example of a more blatant level of abuse among I.R.S. employees.

The Martinezes have the unfortunate distinction of being involved in a tax audit situation turned IRS agent conspiracy. They were already in tax trouble long before they ever walked into the auditor's Laguna Niguel cubicle. What honestly lay at the heart of the Martinezes' tax trouble may never be revealed, but the behavior of the I.R.S. agents assigned to this case speaks volumes about the anatomy of unwarranted I.R.S. tax trouble.

According to the Martinezes, the original I.R.S. office auditor laughed at them and otherwise verbally demeaned them during the examination. The Martinezes came to me after the auditor disallowed all of the personal and business deductions taken on their 1992 and 1993 tax returns.

The first order of business for me was to audit the Martinezes' tax records using the methods and procedures that should have been used by the I.R.S. auditor. The Martinezes' tax records substantiated deducting from their taxable income even more than had been deducted on their original tax returns.

I contacted the auditor and faxed her a copy of my power of attorney.

My examination of the taxpayers' records and my initial contact with the auditor convinced me that the taxpayers' interests would be best served by getting a second opinion from an appeals officer. The auditor's application of the tax laws was, to me, clearly based on subjective factors, most likely racial bias, and had nothing to do with proper I.R.S. procedure. The auditor's already procedurally incorrect behavior turned criminal when she deliberately ignored the taxpayers' request for an appeal. She closed the Martinezes' case *unagreed* and sent it along an administrative channel towards having her opinion of the Martinezes' income tax liability assessed.

Once a tax liability is assessed, it becomes much more difficult procedurally to protest or correct.

The auditor obviously assumed the Martinezes would be ignorant of proper procedures—or, quite possibly, was herself ignorant of the means the taxpayers still had at their disposal to correct the effects of agent misconduct. Normally, once a notice of deficiency has been issued by the I.R.S. to a taxpayer, the only options available to the recipient are to pay the tax or to petition the tax courts. A safeguard procedure is in place which can be used to correct the effects of actions taken by an I.R.S. agent who has abused his or her power. It is called the **audit reconsideration**.

Audit reconsideration can be requested by a taxpayer once a notice of deficiency has been issued formalizing a new tax liability. An audit reconsideration is appropriate and available to taxpayers who were not able to present documentation to an auditor during the normal initial course of the tax audit. There has to be a good reason the taxpayers were not able to present their documentation to the original auditor. The Martinezes' circumstances at the hands of the abusing auditor qualified easily—but not for the reason you might think. The reason the Martinezes qualified to have another auditor take a look at their tax circumstances and records is that the original auditor made a technical mistake by not forwarding the Martinez case to I.R.S. appeals. The request was made verbally. Even though a verbal request is legal and acceptable in an office audit, the written request strengthens the paper trail for the more cautious infighter.

Apparently the auditor thought if she ignored the taxpayer's verbal request for an appeal and did not document the file accordingly there would be no way these people would know how to get out of their trouble. Or, at best, she might have actually forgotten the taxpayers requested an appeal and did not write it down. Such poor job performance still has the net effect of abusing the taxpayers.

In the interview for the Martinezes' audit reconsideration, the auditor did allow the Martinezes many of their correct deductions that were incorrectly disallowed by the original auditor. Their tax liability was being lowered considerably by the I.R.S., but it still was not corrected. I was ready to sing the praises of the I.R.S. as a system. Then the second auditor did a mysterious thing. She staunchly refused to review any of the additional documentation and expenses contained in the taxpayer's records. Again, either this auditor acted on some misguided code of silence—and knew her actions were wrong—or, perhaps worse, she was not familiar enough with the I.R.S. procedure which allows taxpayers under audit to bring in additional documentation for expenses which were not part of the original tax return.

The second auditor's refusal to follow the I.R.S. code and procedures caused a new notice of deficiency to be issued against the Martinezes.

To continue the fight without incurring the additional headaches of lawsuits in tax or civil courts, an Offer in Compromise was filed to counter the effects of this second auditor's tax law misapplications.

An Offer in Compromise can be filed for only one of two possible reasons: doubt as to collectability, meaning the taxpayer can't possibly pay the amount, or doubt as to liability, meaning the taxpayer does not believe they owe the tax liability. The taxpayers must be able to prove either basis for making an Offer In Compromise with their tax records.

That should not have been a problem in the Martinezes' case because they had excellent records to verify not owing the tax liability.

The Martinezes' case found its way into the I.R.S. appeals as a result of the Offer in Compromise. However, this is where the most blatant abuses of the Martinezes occurred.

The Martinezes and I met with an appeals officer. The appeals officer expressed her views on the nature and deductibility of the Martinezes' rental expense based on her individual business practices while operating her own rental property. That was when I first suspected there could be trouble with her judgment of the taxpayers' circumstances. I did not, however, expect a blatantly criminal act to occur while this appeals officer was in possession of the Martinezes' tax records.

Front-line I.R.S. agents would not generally risk acts such as destroying a taxpayer's records unless they felt confident of being able to bury their actions so deep into the system as to never become visible to the taxpayers involved. A degree of confidence in being able to have the support of management is necessary too because the appeals officer is directly supervised by an associate chief of appeals. Surprisingly to me, an additional appeals officer was assigned to the case who offered the Martinezes 70% of their additional rental deductions. This was not acceptable in the Martinezes' circumstances because the taxpayers were 100% entitled to the deductions even though a part of their records had mysteriously disappeared. When records are incomplete due to circumstances beyond the taxpayer's control, the tax code allows for the reconstruction of the taxpayer's records based on remaining information available. Technically, the Martinezes' Offer in Compromise should have been 100% acceptable. Yet the case is now on its way to I.R.S. national office for technical advice—a provision available to taxpayers who believe a district or regional office has misapplied tax laws or I.R.S. procedures to a case.

**Technical advice** is another systemic safeguard which counters the effect of the original auditor's interference with the Martinezes' right to petition the tax court. It can be requested at any point along the path of an audit when the taxpayer suspects that the I.R.S. auditor is in over his or her head on a technical issue, the issues involved are unusual or complex, or there is a demonstrable lack of uniformity in the application of the tax codes or regulations by I.R.S. agents. The operative word in getting out of unwarranted tax trouble is *fight*. As long as you are right and are willing to fight, the system is designed so that you never have to lose because some I.R.S. agent decides to abuse the agency's power.

How many times have you been entitled to a tax deduction but decided against taking it because you were afraid the I.R.S. might audit you? I've got some bad news for you. They might audit you anyway. Just like being good without being real won't save your soul, cheating yourself out of a legitimate tax deduction won't get you into the good graces of the I.R.S.

The I.R.S. randomly selects a number of tax returns, every four or five years, to examine in what they call TCMP (Taxpayer Compliance Measurement Project) audits. It is with what they find on these TCMP audits that the I.R.S. establishes the criteria for choosing that luckless 1% or so of taxpaying Americans who receive audit invitations. Although the tax returns selected for TCMP audits are randomly chosen, these returns face far more scrutiny than normal tax audits. In a regular tax audit the auditor is limited in the number of items on your tax return that can be examined. The TCMP Audit requires the auditor to thoroughly examine every item on the tax return. So even if you dismiss a perfectly legitimate deduction because you're afraid of being audited, you could still be faced with the worst kind of audit. The good news recently out of Washington is that the I.R.S. has suspended the TCMP audits that were scheduled to begin in November 1995.

Consistently, people I encounter who are in tax trouble are afraid of having to deal with the I.R.S. Like I said earlier, the I.R.S. itself doesn't try to instill fear in honest taxpayers. The system tries to encourage voluntary compliance with the tax laws. This way they don't have to hire people to go out and break legs to collect taxes.

## How to Take On the I.R.S. and Win

The way out of tax trouble can be smooth or rough depending on whether you approach your circumstances from a position of fear or of understanding. Fear gives rise to prejudice, hate, street gangs, poverty and higher taxes. Understanding brings about tolerance, love, self-esteem, prosperity and lower income taxes.

Do you panic whenever you see a police officer? Not unless you're a criminal. The only people who have good reason to fear the I.R.S. are those who try to get some tax break they don't legitimately deserve. To be sure, we live in a violent, dangerous society. But to be afraid of another human being because of the job they do, unless their job happens to be armed robber or carjacker, is ridiculous. There is no good reason to be afraid of an I.R.S. agent or situation if you've not done anything deliberately wrong.

## Anatomy of Tax Trouble

Interactions with the I.R.S. might be like ATM banking transactions if they only involved issues of tax law and I.R.S. procedure. Computers can be taught tax law and I.R.S. procedure. But income taxes are based on human behavior and its resultant circumstances. What complicates most tax liability issues is the I.R.S agent's or the taxpayer's misinterpretation of the circumstances. If you earn income, you pay taxes on the portion of your income that exceeds your expenses, deductions and other tax incentives for trying to earn the money. If you lose money while trying to make money, the government pats you on the back with risk incentives and says you don't pay taxes on any money you lost while trying to earn money.

The taxpayer's official statement of his or her tax circumstances is the tax return. When the I.R.S. decides to challenge your statement, by examining the records you present to support it, they may come up with their own interpretation of your circumstances. I don't know of any computer programs that can follow the complexities of human behavior better than the human mind. Apparently the I.R.S. feels the same way because all of their audits and determinations of tax liabilities are done by people.

An audit can be like walking a tightrope across a cage of angry pit bulls. Balance is the only thing that can save you. The balance which must be struck when interacting with an I.R.S. agent is between the agent's observable emotional state and the impression of trustworthiness you project. If the agent doesn't trust you or your paper trail, it justifies his making your way more difficult. If you don't trust an I.R.S. agent and can document a basis for such distrust, you should inform the employee's supervisor. If you suspect the supervisor is trying to cover the employee, go to the supervisor's supervisor.

Although you might be up to your ears in tax trouble, the I.R.S. has to operate within the framework of the tax laws the same as you do. Dealings with I.R.S. agents are like a chess match. The one who is the most resourceful, within the rules, wins.

How to Take On the I.R.S. and Win

# III
# The Human Side of the I.R.S.

This chapter concerns the character of the I.R.S. agents the public must deal with.

I.R.S. agents and you have one thing always in common: *humanness*. To find it or to relate to it may not be a pleasant or easy task. Respecting someone has absolutely nothing to do with liking them. Sometimes liking a person can interfere with genuinely seeing them for who they are.

The I.R.S. relies totally on the judgment calls of its employees when it comes down to decisions regarding tax liability.

We've discussed the unwritten rules and some ideas on how to play the income tax game effectively.

Our attention in this segment will be focused on the players you're likely to encounter on the other team. The next case will illustrate why this is important.

We were already three hours into the audit and my examination of the taxpayer's documents revealed there was no attempt to defraud. But there were clearly some questionable deductions taken on the tax return. By this time in the audit I was baffled because the representative was still red-faced and sweating profusely.

"Are you all right?" I asked him.

He nearly jumped out of his seat. "Oh, I'm all right. My nervous system just goes haywire at these things."

I tried to lighten things up some. "The horse breeding Schedule C is B.S." I smiled. "Your taxpayer's equestrian certificate is for an amateur, which means she cannot compete as a professional. If you'll agree to that adjustment, I won't go any deeper into the return."

Composing himself, he asked, "How much will that cost my client?"

"Seven thousand. Plus penalty and interest."

"Whew! That's a lot." He wiped his brow.

"Not as much as it might cost if I keep examining this tax return." I stopped smiling and again looked through the tax return. "These contributions look pretty high to me."

His sweating intensified.

"O.K. I'll sign."

Actually, he gave up too easily. This, from an I.R.S. point of view, was a quality audit. It had been a first-interview closure with a substantial signed agreement. The unwritten I.R.S. auditor's philosophy, except in the case of obvious fraud or negligence, is to go for the *fast buck*, not the *last buck*.

If this representative had chosen to appeal my decision, he could have dragged the case out through at least a half-dozen more I.R.S. employees. This could cause any adjustments in favor of the I.R.S. to be reduced by the appellate process.

The taxpayer's representative felt good because he had gotten a compromise. I felt good because all I was after was a quick, satisfactory settlement and a closed case. This whole scenario might have ended differently had the representative not responded to my hint of a compromise. Actually, the reason I was so considerate was that I had three other audits scheduled that day and was really pressed for time. If the representative had not seized the compromise opportunity, I would have been forced to make his case a priority and thoroughly examine the taxpayer's records.

An I.R.S. auditor has to excel at high-pressure sales. You did know it was a sales job, didn't you? How else could an auditor get you to agree to pay the government a wad of money for taxes you don't believe you owe?

One of the first things an auditor is supposed to tell you is that you don't have to accept his or her decision as the last word about what you owe the I.R.S. After all, the I.R.S.'s position, at this point, is little more than the agent's opinion of your circumstances. Unless the auditor has you dead wrong and you know it, the auditor's idea of your tax liability is, at best, their opinion. Tax liability, like beauty, is in the eye of the beholder.

I.R.S. notices are an important link in the chain of events that can cause encounters with I.R.S. employees to go badly.

A client recently came to me because the I.R.S. had levied his income. I'll call this client Case 41. Case 41 filed his 1990 tax return but did not pay the taxes due with the return. He had every intention of paying what he owed but... The I.R.S. began sending him a series of notices which he chose to ignore, hoping the whole thing would just go away. It wouldn't go away for him and it won't for you.

The I.R.S. is one of the nation's largest law enforcement agencies. Yet only a small minority of I.R.S. agents actually carry lethal weapons. The rest rely on the tax codes, enormous powers of decision-making and their humanity.

The I.R.S. agents you want to communicate with are the ones who deal with the public when the early notices come. As the number and frequency of I.R.S. notices increases, your chance of solving your problem in a favorable manner decreases.

Worst of all, the personality traits of the agents you'll deal with will more likely be troublesome and they'll be less responsive to a good sob story. *Never ignore I.R.S. notices!*

It is difficult to win with the I.R.S. when a taxpayer has ignored notices to the point of I.R.S.'s collection agents trying to collect on a past due account. Difficult but not impossible. When assets are about to be seized, which is where Case 41 found himself, the I.R.S. informs the taxpayer, offering still another opportunity to resolve the situation amicably.

I filed an Offer In Compromise for Case 41, to get Case 41 back into the hands of a customer service oriented Appeals Officer. To Collection officers, if you've ignored notices it means you've blown opportunities to negotiate what happens to you or your assets.

The Appeals Officer who called me about Case 41 sounded reasonable. I could tell he was at least opening the encounter up on the people level when he made a joke, however dry, about my business name.

"I.R.S. Troubleshooter. What's the trouble?"

"I beg your pardon?" I didn't get it.

"You're an I.R.S. Troubleshooter. I just want to know what the trouble is?" He didn't laugh. He didn't say anything else.

Then it occurred to me that he was trying to be funny, so I laughed. By the end of our phone conversation I was already assured that my position was going to be considered on what evidence I could produce to prove Case 41's losses.

I could help Case 41 because when we first talked, he jokingly compared the I.R.S. to a man who swindled him out of some money.

"When did this happen?" I asked.

"In 1987. If I ever find the son of a bitch I'm going

to stitch his balls to the back of his knees."

I spilled some coffee from my cup.

"What happened?" I asked after I cleaned up the spill. "Can you prove it actually happened? How much money was it?"

"Gosh. I don't know." I could sense he was hesitant to talk about it. So I paraphrased I.R.S. Regulation Section 1.165-8(d) and I.R.S. Code Section 165(e).

"If you've had money stolen from you through embezzlement or misrepresentation, it's a deductible theft loss in the year you discover the theft." He was still reluctant to talk about it.

"I know you might be embarrassed about this but it could be important," I said.

Case 41 took a deep breath and slowly let it out. "He got me for close to a hundred thousand."

"How did he rip you off for so much money?"

"He was supposed to open and manage a specialty clinic for me. I knew nothing about business management and this guy was supposed to be an expert."

The Human Side of the I.R.S.

"When did you find out you weren't going to get your money back?"

"In 1990. That was when I tried to sue him but couldn't find the bastard to serve the papers."

"Yes!!" I punched my fist into the air.

"What's going on?" he asked with a confused expression.

"A hundred thousand dollar above the line theft loss for 1990 means you owe the I.R.S. zilch! They owe you money. Are you sure you can prove this?"

"I have the paperwork and cancelled checks." Case 41 still wasn't clear on what I meant. "What does what you said mean, in English?"

It meant that Case 41 had a deductible theft loss of one hundred thousand dollars, which far and away offset his $12,000 tax liability. He didn't owe the I.R.S. The I.R.S. owed him money.

I.R.S. agents tend to differ in personality according to their functions. I.R.S. public interaction employees operate the **Collections, Examination, Criminal Investigation** and **Inspection Divisions**. If you're playing the game by the rules you never have to put up with anything but courteous professional service from every I.R.S. employee you encounter.

Like I said earlier, you've got to know the other team's players if you're going to play the game to win. Even if you hire someone to actually confront the I.R.S. on your behalf, it's wise to have the lay of the land yourself.

So here, according to function, are those seemingly enigmatic I.R.S. agents.

**Collection Division**

Case 41 was my first experience as a Troubleshooter with I.R.S. employees who answer the phones when a taxpayer's property has been liened or levied. I never encountered any of these people when I worked for the agency but they are some of the most frequent ones I encounter in my private practice.

The employee you're most likely to encounter from Collection Division will be a **Revenue Officer**. Revenue Officers are sometimes college graduates. They are, relatively speaking, well paid compared to some of the other public contact employees. Their annual salaries range from the low twenties to the high fifties.

These are the people who go out and knock on the public's doors trying to collect past due taxes. They are not typically insensitive but many do seem to have a rougher edge to their personalities than other public contact agents.

Revenue Officers are receptive to genuine hardship cases and have been known to do whatever possible to help a taxpayer who has been unfairly caught in the wheels of the system.

Revenue Officers are not required to have any knowledge of tax law beyond how it relates to collection actions such as seizing assets. So they probably couldn't help you if they wanted to when it comes to offering alternative tax strategy solutions.

Revenue Officers can really be hard-nosed if your case causes them a lot of work to collect from you. The easier you make their job for them the better it goes for you.

It does no good to plead the merits of your case to the I.R.S. agent sent to collect from you. Their marching orders do not include being concerned if the amount they are trying to collect is legally correct. Nor can they change a tax determinations once it has been set, even if they believe it to be wrong. This does not mean they can't arrange to have your case returned to other agents who can change tax liabilities. But to engineer this requires raw people skills.

The next story deals with one way to stay out of major harm even if you're confronted with a particularly difficult Revenue Officer.

I got involved in Case 349 when the situation started to turn ugly.

The Human Side of the I.R.S.

Case 349 was a close acquaintance who casually mentioned having some problems trusting the Revenue Officer (R.O.) assigned to collect from her corporation. Case 349 had on a previous occasion hinted at expecting trouble with this particular R.O. She commented about verbal agreements the R.O. made with her then either forgot or changed his mind about. She was afraid to trust him and hired me to negotiate a repayment agreement with the I.R.S. on her behalf.

"I need copies of any paperwork you have from this Revenue Officer," I told Case 349. The first order of business with any I.R.S. situation is to determine the status of the case in the I.R.S. system. A case to the point of asset seizure requires immediate action, such as an ATAO; to stop them, whereas a case with an agent conducting an investigation prior to deciding on the I.R.S.'s course of collection action leaves room for creative resolution strategies.

Case 349's paperwork from the Revenue Officer I'll call Mr. Shore indicated he was conducting an investigation to establish the I.R.S.'s collection strategy with Case 349. The Revenue Officer had the power to set in motion a reasonable repayment agreement or enforced collection activities. Enforced collection activities include liens, levies, seizures and sales of assets.

I called Mr. Shore on the phone after having faxed a copy of my Power of Attorney to him. Revenue Officers hate to deal with taxpayer representatives. They think we get in their way and gum up the system with delaying tactics. The Revenue Officer's performance is appraised in large measure by the number of cases closed quickly.

I tried to make him feel a bit more comfortable by telling him I had been an auditor.

Mr. Shore suddenly took on a condescending tone. "Oh. But having been in Examination you probably aren't very familiar with the Collection side of the I.R.S."

*You presumptuous a— e,* I thought. But I kept my mouth shut and let him talk. He seemed to take my lack of a response as a sign of weakness because his tone became grandiose.

"I could assess the one hundred percent penalty against your taxpayer or go for enforced sale of her corporation's assets."

I knew he was just trying to get a closed case as quickly as he could, but it was a real struggle to remain civil. But civil doesn't mean wimpy.

"I'm not worried about the penalty and I would stop any of your enforcement actions with ATAO, an Offer In Compromise or a Congressional. So can we get down to what it takes to set up a satisfactory repayment agreement?"

Mr. Shore outlined what Case 349 would need to do in order to get a repayment agreement in place. I immediately laid out the conditions as I understood them in a letter which I forwarded certified to Mr. Shore. Establishing a paper trail is critical to winning against the I.R.S. My conversation with Mr. Shore convinced me that I had better cover my client's rear end with a paper trail that could prevent Mr. Shore from pulling further cowboy antics on Case 349.

A sufficient paper trail documents my actions and my understanding of the agent's actions. Saying one thing and seeming to have forgotten what was said later is a sign that the I.R.S. agent's paper trail is weak. If a tax situation ever goes as far as tax court, the strongest documentation wins.

In situations with unpaid employment taxes, tactics such as those which were being employed by Mr. Shore are designed to psychologically strong-arm the taxpayer into quick payment. Revenue Officers usually feel no sympathy for people who don't pay employment taxes because the money for taxes is withheld from the salaries of employees. The employees and the government trust the employer to collect and pay over to the I.R.S. funds collected for the payment of employment taxes. Hence, the name of the 100% penalty—the Trust Fund Recovery Act Penalty. Revenue Officers tend to get bent out of shape when employers use trust funds to pay other business expenses to keep a venture afloat. But, fortunately for Case 349, this had not been the circumstances.

## The Human Side of the I.R.S.

Case 349's circumstances demonstrated that the non-payment of the taxes did not stem from willful acts for which Case 349 was responsible. Mr. Shore's paper trail would eventually show that he had not sufficiently explored these circumstances.

Mr. Shore had demonstrated in five minutes on the phone an annoying tendency towards prejudging people and circumstances—traits which call into question his integrity.

Lack of integrity is a big deal for an I.R.S. agent. It is grounds for disciplinary actions against an agent up to and including dismissal from the I.R.S. This could prove disastrous to the government's case in appeals or in tax court.

I wrote a letter to Mr. Shore's supervisors complaining about his treatment of Case 349 and of myself and sent a copy to the Inspection Division. Inspection Division is the I.R.S. equivalent of Police Internal Affairs. Then I requested copies of Case 349's entire administrative file from the I.R.S. Disclosure Office under the Freedom of Information Act of 1974.

The reason for going directly through the Disclosure Office if you suspect the agent you're dealing with has an integrity problem is that it lessens the chances the agent will have the time or the opportunity to alter his documentation.

Mr. Shore's administrative file proved to be a virtual gold mine of improperly researched and undocumented actions.

Mr. Shore, in his quest for a fast resolution to the case, was in fact inappropriately harassing Case 349.

His own documentation would be the most effective weapon to prove our case against the I.R.S.

All I.R.S. Agents must justify what they do by documenting any actions taken with evidence and relevant tax code citings.

There is no way the I.R.S. can defend decisions based on a sloppy investigation or inadequate research and documentation by an Agent.

Eventually, Mr. Shore's supervisors began trying to cover for his sloppy work by allowing Mr. Shore to threaten Case 349 with immediate enforcement action.

It was time to use our paper trail.

I was able to convince one of Mr. Shore's Division Chiefs that my paper trail was strong enough to initiate a Congressional investigation or a lawsuit for damages, all based on the inconsistencies in Mr. Shore's behavior and documentation and the series of letters I had written to him, his management, and the Inspection Division.

A repayment agreement was quickly executed by Mr. Shore for Case 349.

**Examination Division**

The Examination Division of the I.R.S. consists of public contact employees who determine and assess tax liability. To accomplish this they use a variety of tax law and procedural resources. But most importantly, they use their own judgment to make decisions about you, your representative and your tax records.

There are essentially two kinds of auditors, office

and field auditors. Office auditors handle individual and small business cases which fall at or below one million dollars of income. Revenue Agents or field auditors handle individuals, partnerships, trusts, corporations, small and large business audits. Auditors are far more likely than other I.R.S. agents to have come to their job from some other career or profession. A good number of lawyers, waiting to pass state bar exams, are tax auditors.

The economy of a given time and community determines the types of people you encounter as I.R.S. auditors.

In less densely populated, rural areas, their numbers consist largely of people who have come up through the ranks of other I.R.S. Divisions, usually Taxpayer's Service.

In large cities like Los Angeles, you're more likely to encounter highly educated auditors who are riding out bad economic times in other careers with a secure government job. There are also career civil servants.

The tax auditor is the target of much of the public's fear of I.R.S. agents. Auditors can also be wellsprings of good I.R.S. procedural information. Salaries for auditors range from the low twenties to the upper fifties. Auditors are among the most open-minded public access I.R.S. employees. Their job gives them the power to, without your permission, obtain otherwise private information about you. An encounter with an auditor is where you are the most likely to come upon an empathetic I.R.S. employee—one where human relationship skills will reap the most benefits.

Many hold the common misconception that if they don't have complete records to verify a tax deduction, the I.R.S. auditor will automatically disallow it. Not true. Approximations, reconstruction and oral testimony are acceptable means of verifying items in an audit.

In an audit situation, establishing credibility through your records is the key to making the auditor see you as human. The auditor can then feel comfortable enough with you to allow the use of oral testimony, reconstruction or approximations to verify an otherwise unverifiable expense or deduction.

*Approximations* are exactly what their name implies, your very best guess at the amount of a given deduction or expense. Typically you must be able to verify similar items of expense or deduction with complete documentation on prior or subsequent tax returns. This helps to establish in the auditor's mind the likelihood of similar expenses or deductions occurring in the year for which you lack adequate documentation.

*Reconstruction* involves creating substitute records to replace missing ones. The agent should be told, up front, when records have been reconstructed. Should the auditor discover in the course of an examination that a journal substantiating miles was not created at or close to the time of the event for which a deduction is taken, your credibility can become questionable in the auditor's mind.

Once you've been able to convince the auditor that a deduction is *ordinary*, meaning that anyone else doing the same or similar business would have a similar expense, then the item must be seen by the auditor as *necessary* to your trade or business or job in some way.

**Reasonableness** is what the auditor will seek to understand next about your tax circumstances. There are no laws against stupidity when it comes to conducting business, but the auditor must be convinced that what you did was, to you, a reasonable attempt to make money. To say to an auditor that you took a guest to the Bahamas because you needed to get away and think about your business might seem perfectly reasonable to you. But you might have a hard time convincing an I.R.S. employee that the costs for the trip and your guest are a reasonable business expense. However, if trips like this are a part of the mix that makes you and your business work, all expenses for such a junket are tax deductible.

Lastly, the auditor must be convinced the item was *paid for* by you. How you accomplish this is limited only by your own creativity.

*Oral testimony* involves getting an auditor to take you at your word without any documentation to back it up. It's done a lot more often than you might think. Being an alluring member of the opposite sex of the auditor cannot always be counted upon to engender this kind of blind trust. (But if it works...) Usually it is accomplished when the auditor has seen some prior documented evidence that establishes your credibility as a historian. Even if the initial auditor does not buy your oral testimony, you may get to try your luck with other auditors, managers, appeals officers or the tax court.

I can think of six ideas which can enhance your ability to appeal to the human side of I.R.S. auditors:

**(1) Don't put off your appointment.** To continuously put off your appointment is probably the worst single piece of advice I've ever heard given to taxpayers who are scheduled to be audited. When an audit appointment is assigned, the auditor is likely to only glance at the case before the scheduled interview appointment. Auditors must account for their time daily.

If you don't show up for your scheduled appointment, the auditor is forced to use the time that was slated to be spent with you or your representative examining the case for whatever appears suspicious on the return. The auditor will then disallow every questionable deduction. If you or your representative are not there to influence the auditor's judgment, everything about you becomes questionable. What might have originally been limited to examining a few items on a tax return can turn into a TCMP-like audit where every item on the return is being challenged. Penalties and interest are also added. At this point, the laws which govern the I.R.S. part company with the way American criminal laws operate. The auditor does not have to prove you are guilty. You have to prove you are innocent.

**(2) Be yourself.** Unless you happen to have a particularly abrasive personality. Then it's best if you hire someone to show up with you or for you.

The auditor from the outset is paying attention,

not only to what you have to say, but to how you are saying it—and to what you are *not* saying. Genuineness goes a long way towards establishing credibility.

According to I.R.S. training, the auditor is supposed to take control of the audit. Let them. If you try to take the initiative, you force the auditor into a contest of wills.

**(3) Watch out for self-incrimination**. There is no constitutional protection here against putting your own foot in your mouth. The agent will most likely use the tactic of asking you open-ended questions. It's a psychological fishing expedition. It might be to your advantage to ask for clarification, effectively closing those open-ended questions.

**(4) Pay attention** to the surroundings. The auditor's manner of dress, desk and cubicle decorations can lead you to notice things you and the auditor might have in common. It also might help you discover what to avoid in relating to this human being.

**(5) Don't lie**. If any I.R.S. employee catches you in a lie, your credibility goes out the window, usually along with any tendency to be charitable on the part of the I.R.S. employee.

**(6) Don't despair.** If an audit decision goes against you, the auditor's judgment does not have to be the last word on the matter.

Every new I.R.S. employee must consent to three years of personal tax audits, called employee audits, as a part of their background investigation. In my employee audit the auditor disallowed an alimony and a moving expense deduction on my return. I had to fight for it but through reconstruction, oral testimony and an appeals hearing, I was ultimately able to win a reversal of the auditor's decision.

Remember, these people are human beings. Unless the taxpayer's records are blatantly fraudulent, the auditor will most likely be willing to negotiate a settlement in the case. Actually, many tax fraud cases go without ever being prosecuted as such. An auditor has to go above and beyond the call of duty to develop a tax fraud case. Come on! We're talking about government employees here! The typical auditor would rather have a root canal done than go through all of the work necessary to have a case considered for fraud prosecution.

C.I.D., Inspection and some Revenue agents take to tax fraud a lot more aggressively than do tax auditors. Your chances of being pursued for tax fraud do increase with your social status or name recognition. The I.R.S. depends on the public's voluntary compliance with tax laws. They jump at the chance for some celebrity to cross the line into noncompliance, or better yet, tax evasion.

It's a good idea to know whether or not the office auditor you deal with is a business auditor or a junior auditor. There is a difference in the kind of information a business auditor and a junior auditor can demand from you. For example, a junior auditor, in an office audit, should not request to examine your bank deposits, cost of goods sold, or records of gross receipts. Business auditors have pretty much a free hand in the kinds of records they can examine and request from you, except that business auditors cannot examine records or returns concerning corporations or partnerships.

Revenue agents, Inspection and C.I.D. Agents are able to examine any type of return or taxpayer records.

*Problems Resolution Office*

The Problems Resolution Office is frequently staffed by temporarily assigned auditors. These examiners view an assignment to the Problems Resolution Office as a respite from the trenches of doing audits. Their functions are to resolve assessment problem situations which stem from disputes between taxpayers and I.R.S. employees. They are also charged sometimes with cleaning up problems which result from personality conflicts between I.R.S. Agents.

The circumstances Problems Resolution will attempt to resolve must meet certain criteria. To put it succinctly, you must have exhausted all other means of resolving the problem situation within the I.R.S.

The advantage of dealing with examiners in Problems Resolution is that you have an auditor who has no emotional attachment to the case.

## *Appeals Officers*

Suppose you disagree with an auditor's decision and decide to exercise your right to appeal. Dig in for a long wait. It's likely to take as long as six months before you're ever contacted by an Appeals Officer about your case.

Appeals Officers are frequently former audit group managers who've obtained promotions to positions in Appeals. It's the Appeals Officer's call whether or not the I.R.S. stands to win or lose against you in front of a tax court judge. If the Appeals Officer thinks you have a case strong enough to possibly sway a judge's decision against the I.R.S., watch how fast the I.R.S. starts trying to strike a deal with you. The *fast buck* not the *last buck*, remember?

The only way a case gets to the appellate level to begin with, supposedly, is if the auditor has researched the law and documented a case well enough for the I.R.S. to defend in court if necessary.

The Appeals Officer represents the best deal you're likely to get from the I.R.S. If you can't strike a deal with the Appeals Division, get ready to go to tax court. If a case reaches the courts, judges have no reputation for loyalty to the I.R.S.

## *Taxpayer Service*

Taxpayer Service Specialists must have a Bachelor's degree, four years of college study, three years of appropriate professional experience, or an equivalent combination of education and experience. Some are incredibly knowledgeable and helpful. But for information beyond very basic tax issues the 1-800-1040 number is not the place to call. These are the

I.R.S. employees once tapped for the dubious distinction of giving the public information, which is incorrect 42% of the time. It must be said in their defense that, they are required to answer as many as a thousand calls from the public each day, with a good number of these calls monitored by a supervisor. For their trouble, candidates for Taxpayer Service Specialist can expect to begin their careers at between $18,331 and $22,705 per year.

*Seizing the Moment*

Does the I.R.S. act in its own best interest when they put someone out of business and auction off their assets to recover back taxes? The very assets the taxpayer needs to make a living? You bet! Sometimes such taxpayers are the best P.R. for the I.R.S. that money can buy.

As I outlined earlier, before a tax situation ever gets to the point of the I.R.S. seizing assets to satisfy a tax liability, there have been between six and eight attempts initiated by the I.R.S. to resolve the situation differently. The public sees some famous person being stripped of everything they own except bedding and clothing. The I.R.S., though not as a primary objective, gets a message across to the public about what happens when you owe and don't pay taxes.

It is wise to get the Taxpayer Service Telephone Specialist's name before you begin to discuss your situation. Don't go for the fast garbled salutation when they answer the phone. Get them to slowly give their name and spell it out if you have to. This tends to establish accountability.

Problem situations with these employees can be resolved by insisting on a supervisor's intervention. Proceed here with discretion.

The I.R.S. has in place a procedure to abate penalties which result from misinformation given by an I.R.S. employee.

## *Criminal Investigation Division*

The C.I.D. or Criminal Investigation Division is peopled by some of the best the I.R.S. offers. They are required to be college educated in accounting and business courses. C.I.D. agents are trained in a federal police academy. They carry lethal weapons and all the power the federal government can muster in examining records of suspected tax criminals. Most often they are people you'd never suspect of being criminal investigators. They might follow a suspect around in teams of expensive cars or record that person's every move with a camcorder. The car and the camcorder were most likely confiscated in a drug or tax liability raid and are now in the service of the C.I.D.

I once was suspicious that a taxpayer and his brother were one and the same person. I asked a C.I.D. agent to help me. Within an hour I saw passport-quality pictures of both brothers. That resolved my doubts.

## Inspection Division

What keeps I.R.S. employees from taking bribes? That *other group* of gun-toting I.R.S. Agents—the *Inspection Division*. These agents, when they're not supplementing the Secret Service guarding the President, are keeping an eye on I.R.S. employees to make sure everything is in order.

I.R.S. employees never know when someone trying to solicit a bribe might be an undercover Inspection Agent.

Inspection also investigates when a taxpayer complains of impropriety by an I.R.S. employee.

My only direct encounter with Inspection came when a woman threatened to file a complaint of misconduct against me.

The woman was appearing before me on a power

of attorney as a friend of the taxpayer—perfectly legal and accepted practice since many taxpayers are afraid to deal directly with the I.R.S.

So enticing was the low-cut dress she wore to the audit that male co-workers were finding excuses to walk past my desk to sneak a look. The woman talked freely to me about her father and his obsession with garlic as a curative but not much else. Noticeably absent was any explanation of the taxpayer's deductions.

During my six-year stint with the I.R.S., never was I forced to choose between my libido and the government's money. However, this woman, after being so warm and friendly, called me and threatened to go to my supervisors, saying I tried to put a move on her. She, of course, offered to keep quiet if I would get rid of her friend's tax liability.

I called Inspection and told them how this woman was trying to intimidate me.

A tough-looking, well-dressed guy turned up at

my desk later that day. He flashed his badge and I.D. which revealed his Irish surname. He spoke with a Boston accent and laid his stainless steel briefcase down on my desk. His message was crystal clear from the way he carried himself. If I was dirty, he wouldn't hesitate to burn me.

I was hoping my own non-verbal message, *I'm clean so screw you, tough guy,* came through.

I explained the situation, not leaving out any details. He seemed to accept what I said at face value. Yet I can still see his steel blue eyes and his poker face as he said. "I have to ask you this. Did you hit on her?"

I was straight up.

"No. I wouldn't have kicked her out of bed either. But I didn't hit on her."

I never heard from the woman or Inspection again. Only afterwards did I suspect that she might have been sent by Inspection.

## How All The Pieces Fit Together

Often they don't. Not when it comes to the various types of I.R.S. employees. Auditors don't generally know how Revenue Officers function; Taxpayer Service Specialists don't know much about how Auditors really function. None of the other I.R.S. employees know how C.I.D. or Inspection really function.

This polarization and resultant lack of communication among functions within the system accounts at times for some of the more blatant snafus that I.R.S. personnel create.

The I.R.S. has apparently seen the error of its ways in this regard. As of this writing they are launching internal programs to diminish this revenue-reducing polarization among its employees and functions.

# IV
# WHAT TO DO WHEN AN I.R.S. AGENT FIGHTS DIRTY

Are Rodney King-like incidents ever perpetrated on taxpayers by I.R.S. agents? Unfortunately, yes.

An I.R.S. lawyer erroneously suspects a taxpayer of stalling and using delaying tactics to prevent the I.R.S. from collecting more than one million dollars in back taxes, interest and penalties. The taxpayer's crime? Hiring me to do an independent audit of their tax records, personal and business circumstances. The overzealous I.R.S. lawyer initiates a tax audit of the taxpayers. The I.R.S. lawyer then uses his position to negatively influence Auditors and managerial staff executives in the audit. Sound like fiction? The Carters of Nashville, TN, wish this story were not true. The Carters have lived with the huge dark shadow of the

I.R.S. on them for more than ten years.

In the spring of 1996 I was retained by the Carters to conduct an independent, federal income tax audit on their records and circumstances for the years the I.R.S. had made additional tax assessments. My audit revealed that the taxpayers were due a huge refund from the government for every year between 1986 and 1994.

The chief culprit? The Carters' tax returns did not correctly communicate their business and personal tax circumstances to the I.R.S.

The Carters' tax return information correctly did not trigger the I.R.S. audit machine because they had not underpaid their taxes. The I.R.S. tax codes, treasury regulations and internal revenue manual are designed to guide the human operator of the machine to legally correct decisions and actions. It has been my experience that for the most part this system is fair and works flawlessly when used as directed. Which brings me to the point of this discussion.

The I.R.S. system relies heavily on the judgment of its human agents to move the wheels of tax justice.

## What to Do When an I.R.S. Agent Fights Dirty

The function of this element of the machine is only as good as the agent's judgment. Our legislators are obviously aware that the same distractions which can cloud human judgment in society as a whole can most certainly influence human judgment in law enforcement.

The system works properly when I.R.S. agents know the law they are charged with enforcing. There are cases where the emotional or psychological involvement of a given I.R.S. agent outdistances his or her knowledge of the law. The government has clearly covered itself on this one though. The burden of the proof of innocence rests squarely on the taxpayer's shoulders. The agent is not legally bound to be correct unless you prove the opposite. However, the tax codes provides incredible freedom of tax-sheltered movement for legitimate movers and shakers.

The system is designed to be suspicious only of taxpayers who might not have paid enough. Obviously, the I.R.S. will not assign employees to see if you paid them too much for particular tax-related situations, but the I.R.S. is required to refund your money if you can show you've paid them too much. You've got to show them the money!

In the Carter case, I immediately filed protective claims for refunds from the I.R.S. for the Carters. That was when the real I.R.S. lynch party started.

Prejudice was a major player in the Carters' tax trouble. But the I.R.S. system is designed with checks and balances which are supposed to correct for things like biases. These systemic safeguards dissolve when someone like a district counsel is pulling the strings of lower-ranking district employees. Most of the Nashville district employees involved probably had no clue that they were participating in violations of the Carters' rights.

The I.R.S. lawyer's first step over the line was in a motion to a federal court judge, in which he accused the taxpayers of filing amended tax returns as a ploy to delay the collection of assessed taxes, interest and penalties. The primary problem with the I.R.S. lawyer's suspicion was that he was wrong. But his bum-

## What to Do When an I.R.S. Agent Fights Dirty

bling did not stop with his own mistakes. This "learned" man took his unfounded suspicions to a level I had not previously seen in an I.R.S. employee. Even if his suspicions had been correct, he was required to follow the rules to expose and document the allegations. What in fact ended up being documented and exposed unwittingly in the administrative file was a conspiracy involving underlings of the district counsel pursuing an I.R.S. witch hunt against an innocent taxpayer.

The auditor assigned to the Carters immediately began to fight dirty by extending the unfair treatment of the taxpayer to her examination process. The auditor misapplied several tax laws that should have been understood by someone in her position. Initially, she deliberately participated in a conspiracy to block the transfer of the case to California. By law, the I.R.S. is mandated to transfer a case to a district near where the books and records necessary to substantiate the returns are kept. That would be Southern California.

I have stressed earlier the importance of obtaining

the entire administrative file whenever you confront I.R.S. tax trouble. It is the only way you stand a chance of proving your innocence when an agent has played dirty.

The Revenue Agent's workpapers indicate she was a willing participant in a plot among other I.R.S. employees in California's Laguna Niguel and Tennessee's Nashville districts to nullify I.R.S. policy regarding the circumstances that warrant the transfer of a case.

The mistakes and other problems in the Carters' administrative file read like a training aid on detecting an I.R.S. conspiracy. Remember, this was all inspired by one suspicious agent's beliefs. I honestly believe that agents who would stoop to such levels are in the minority.

It takes an incredible amount of integrity to remain objective when enforcing tax laws. Not all agents who otherwise meet the requirements of the job of an I.R.S. agent have reached the emotional and psychological maturity to handle the intense demands of the job. Hence, some I.R.S. agents play dirty when they administer and enforce the tax laws.

By running a business called I.R.S. Troubleshooters, I probably encounter more than a fair share of I.R.S. bad apples.

Often, when an I.R.S. agent has it in for a taxpayer and is in the wrong, the only place you can trip him or her up and break up an unjustified tax lynching is in the administrative file.

So when an I.R.S. agent tells you that you owe the government more than it costs to buy a brand new Rolls Royce, remember, they're all human beings, prone to the same mistakes and errors in judgment as the rest of us. Calmly ask for a copy of the administrative file, which should contain any workpapers (documents) which explain such a pronouncement. You will want to pay strict attention to the agent's paper trail for technical or procedural errors. These kinds of errors are often surprisingly evident under the careful scrutiny of detached analysis. Especially if the agent is playing dirty. Then search the return preparation records and circumstances for tax return communication errors. Many tax troubles disappear when income tax records and circumstances are examined carefully.

# PROFILE

Alexander Howard writes about tax trouble and the mind of the I.R.S. agent with insights gained as a therapist who happened to work as a tax auditor for six years conducting nearly 6,000 I.R.S. audits. Mr. Howard presently owns and operates I.R.S. Troubleshooters, a private tax trouble investigation service based in Southern California.

# How to Take On the I.R.S. and Win

# Some Keys to I.R.S. Administrative File Jargon

AMTS = amounts
BC = Branch Chief
BDA = Bank deposit analysis
BUS = Business
COGS = Cost of goods sold
DC = Division chief
DOC = Document
Fm = form
Grp Mgr = Group manager
LMTCB = Left message to call back
PC = Phone Call
POA = Taxpayer representative
P/R = Per return
RA = Revenue agent
RO = Revenue officer
RTN = Return
TA = Tax auditor
TP = Taxpayer
TPH = Taxpayer husband
TPW = Taxpayer wife